BRIGHT
IDEA
BOOKS

THE
Truth ABOUT
LIFE AS A
U.S. Army Soldier

by M. Kirkman

CAPSTONE PRESS
a capstone imprint

Bright Ideas is published by Capstone Press, an imprint of Capstone.
1710 Roe Crest Drive
North Mankato, Minnesota 56003
www.capstonepub.com

Library of Congress Cataloging-in-Publication Data
Names: Kirkman, M., 1982- author.
Title: The truth about life as a U.S. Army soldier / M. Kirkman.
Description: North Mankato : Capstone Press, [2020] | Series: The real scoop | Includes index. | Audience: Grades 4-6
Identifiers: LCCN 2019029504 (print) | LCCN 2019029505 (ebook) | ISBN 9781543590692 (hardcover) | ISBN 9781543590708 (ebook)
Subjects: LCSH: Soldiers—United States—Juvenile literature. | United States. Army--Military life Juvenile literature. | United States. Army—Vocational guidance—Juvenile literature.
Classification: LCC UA25 .K49 2020 (print) | LCC UA25 (ebook) | DDC 355.1/20973—dc23
LC record available at https://lccn.loc.gov/2019029504
LC ebook record available at https://lccn.loc.gov/2019029505

Image Credits
iStockphoto: DanielBendjy, 24, ollo, 18–19, Pekic, 20–21, PeopleImages, 12–13; Shutterstock Images: Africa Studio, 11, Burlingham, 6–7, michaeljung, 26–27, Presslab, 14, 28, solepsizm, 8–9, wavebreakmedia, cover; U.S. Army: Sgt. Dominique M. Clarke, 504th MI Brigade Public Affairs, 5, Sgt. Erick Yates, Multinational Battle Group-East, 30–31, Spc. Samuel Soza, 23; U.S. Army Reserve: 17
Design Elements: Shutterstock Images

Editorial Credits
Editor: Charly Haley; Designer: Laura Graphenteen; Production Specialist: Dan Peluso

All internet sites appearing in back matter were available and accurate when this book was sent to press.

Printed in the United States of America.
PA99

TABLE OF CONTENTS

CHAPTER 1

THE MANY JOBS
of Soldiers

A soldier watches her computer. She sees that an enemy truck is on the move. She knows where the truck is going. She has watched it for weeks. She is a U.S. Army soldier. She is on the **intelligence** team. Her job keeps other soldiers safe.

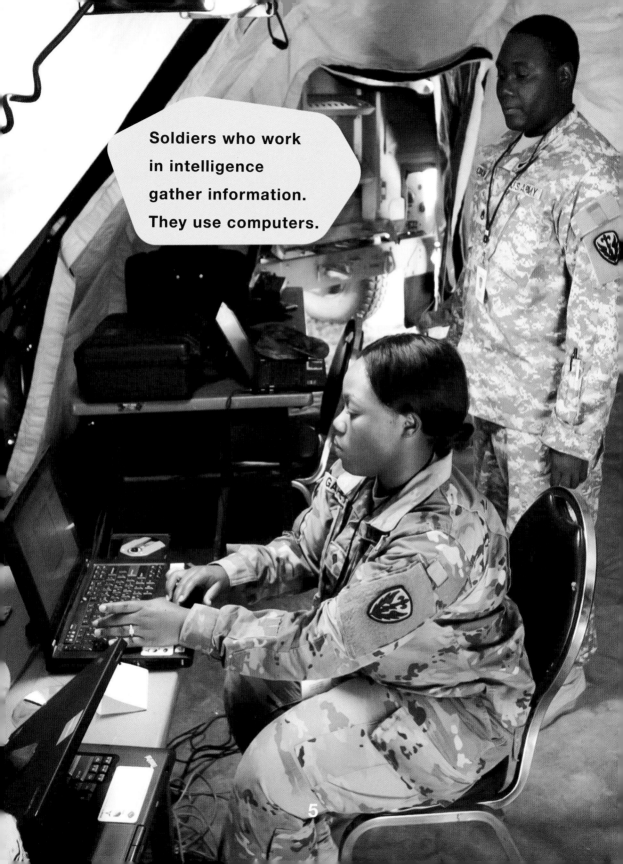

Soldiers who work in intelligence gather information. They use computers.

There are many types of jobs in the U.S. Army. Many different teams work together. Some are **engineers**. They may use **drones** to take pictures of land. Some engineers make maps. Maps help soldiers move safely from place to place.

Other soldiers drive tanks or fix broken equipment. Some send messages. The army also has police and firefighter teams.

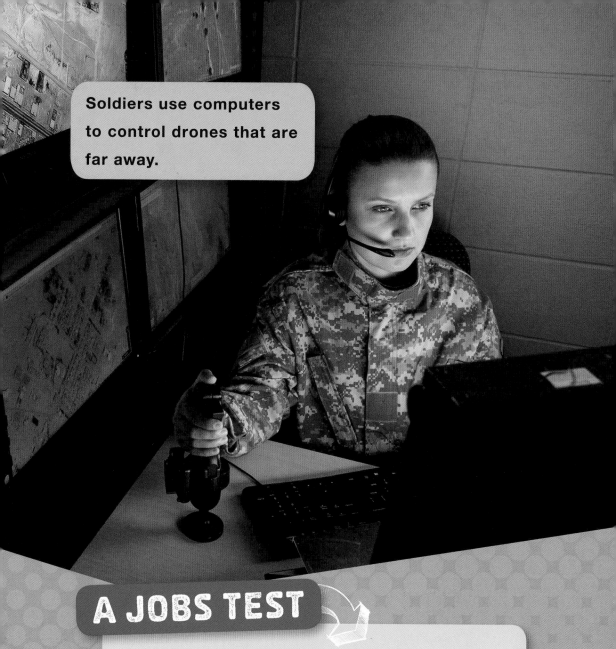

Soldiers use computers to control drones that are far away.

A JOBS TEST

Soldiers take a test when they join the army. It tells them which jobs are best for them.

When big storms damage cities, army soldiers go there to help.

Soldiers guard the country.

In times of war, soldiers fight.

They may go to other countries.

They fight to keep America safe.

Soldiers help in other ways too. Hurricanes and other **natural disasters** put people in danger. Soldiers bring people to safety. They bring supplies to people in need.

CHAPTER 2

JOINING the Army

Some soldiers join the army in college. They join the **Army ROTC**. This means the soldier is in army training and college at the same time. The army helps the soldier pay for college.

BECOMING OFFICERS

Soldiers who join the army through the ROTC become officers. They lead others.

ROTC students have to keep up with their classes and army training.

Other soldiers join the army after high school. They do this instead of going to college. Soldiers must graduate from high school. They must be at least 17 years old.

Soldiers visit schools to see if students are interested in joining.

13

Army soldiers help each other.

ARMY UNIFORMS

Soldiers learn to dress in **uniform** at boot camp. They must wear their hair and clothes in certain ways.

Soldiers begin training in boot camp. This is where soldiers learn to work as a team. They learn how to use **weapons**. Soldiers must learn the rules of the army. Soldiers become strong during boot camp. Boot camp is about 10 weeks long.

CHAPTER 3

THE GOOD AND
the Bad

The U.S. Army guards the country.

It keeps the American people safe.

Soldiers are proud to serve their country.

Soldiers usually serve for two to six years in the army. Some may serve longer. The army helps soldiers get jobs when they leave the army.

Many soldiers join the army because they want to help other Americans.

Army bases are busy.
The U.S. Army has
bases all over the world.

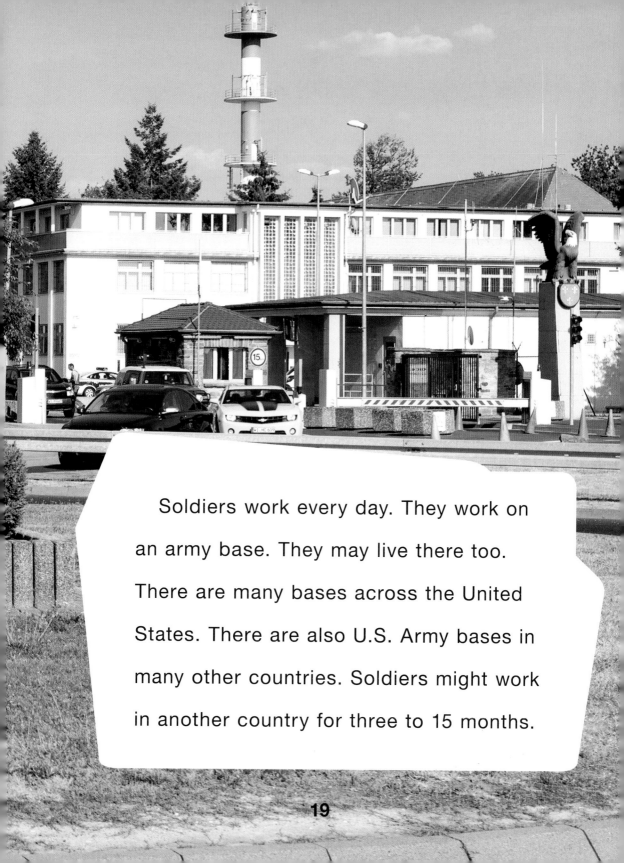

Soldiers work every day. They work on an army base. They may live there too. There are many bases across the United States. There are also U.S. Army bases in many other countries. Soldiers might work in another country for three to 15 months.

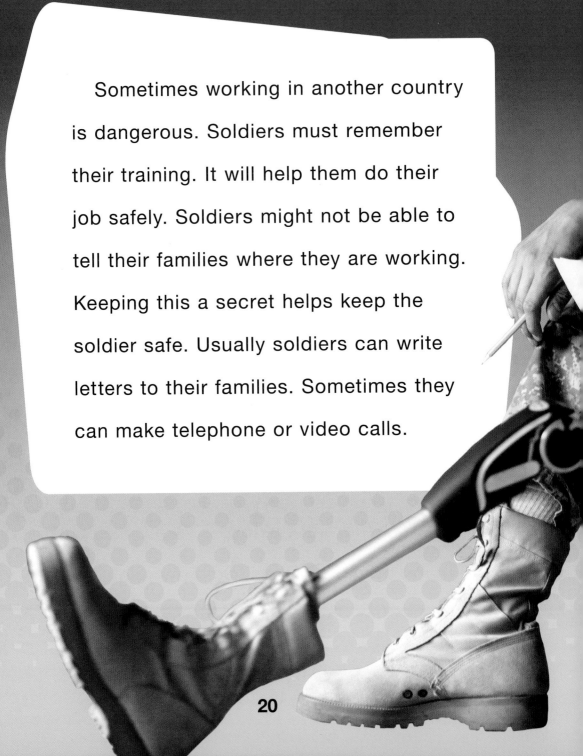

Sometimes working in another country is dangerous. Soldiers must remember their training. It will help them do their job safely. Soldiers might not be able to tell their families where they are working. Keeping this a secret helps keep the soldier safe. Usually soldiers can write letters to their families. Sometimes they can make telephone or video calls.

Writing letters helps many soldiers stay close to their families at home.

CHAPTER 4

LIFE ON a Base

Many soldiers live together on a base. An army base is like a small town. Soldiers visit stores and restaurants. Soldiers also go swimming or play basketball at the gym.

Some bases even have movie theaters and parks. Soldiers sleep in a building called a **barracks**. It is like an apartment building.

There are many ways soldiers can have fun on the base. Some play sports for fun.

Soldiers can live with their families on the base.

Some soldiers are married and have children. A soldier's family can live on the base too. There are apartments and houses for families on the base.

Some bases have schools. Most bases have a library. Military families spend time together. They are just like other families.

U.S. Army soldiers have important jobs. They guard the country and help people. They train a lot and work hard. Sometimes their jobs are dangerous. But they serve their country with pride.

Soldiers work hard, but many are happy to do it to serve their country.

U.S. ARMY

GLOSSARY

Army ROTC
the Army Reserve Officers' Training Corps (ROTC), a program for college students to join the army

barracks
a building or group of buildings where soldiers live

drone
an aircraft that is controlled by a pilot on the ground

engineer
a person whose job it is to design or build

intelligence
information about an enemy or possible enemy. The army's intelligence team learns information about possible enemies to keep people safe.

natural disaster
a sudden and dangerous event in nature that can damage buildings and hurt people, such as a tornado or hurricane

uniform
matching clothing worn by members of a group

TRIVIA

1. **Lieutenant Colonel Theodore Roosevelt** was an army soldier during the Spanish-American War in 1898. Then in 1901 he became the 26th U.S. president.

2. **First Lieutenant Vernon J. Baker** was awarded a U.S. Army Medal of Honor for his heroism in World War II. He was one of seven African American soldiers to receive the honor in 1997, years after the war.

3. Only one woman, **Dr. Mary Walker,** has received an army Medal of Honor. She served as a surgeon during the Civil War.

ACTIVITY

INTERVIEW A U.S. ARMY SOLDIER

Create a list of questions to ask a U.S. Army soldier. You could ask:

1. What is your job in the army?

2. Do you live on the army base? What is your home like?

3. Have you worked for the army in another country?

Think of your own questions too. If you know a soldier, set up a time to talk to him or her. Ask him or her your list of questions. If you don't know a soldier, write a letter. Send your letter to a U.S. Army base. You can find the address online.

FURTHER RESOURCES

Want to learn more about the U.S. Army?
Check out these resources:

Otfinoski, Steven. *U.S. Army True Stories: Tales of Bravery*. North Mankato, Minn.: Capstone Press, 2015.

USO: Army Trivia Facts
https://www.uso.org/stories/1546-33-military-facts-that-may-surprise-you

Interested in other parts of the military?
Check out these books:

Leavitt, Amie Jane. *U.S. Navy by the Numbers*. North Mankato, Minn.: Capstone Press, 2014.

Shank, Carol. *U.S. Military Weapons and Artillery*. North Mankato, Minn.: Capstone Press, 2013.

INDEX